CONGRA[...] [...]ol,

ON you[...]

work in our Go-to-

Church Club..

Your BOOK WAS

Chosen as The Best

Among the 9-year

Girls.

Thornton William

PASOr

5-2-1968

D0810633

A GIRL'S BOOK OF PRAYERS

By John Lewis Sandlin

A PRAYER FOR EVERY DAY

GRACES AND PRAYERS

MOMENTS WITH THE MASTER

A BOOK OF TABLE GRACES

A PRAYER FOR EVERY MEETING

A BOOK OF PRAYERS FOR YOUTH

A GIRL'S BOOK OF PRAYERS

A BOY'S BOOK OF PRAYERS

A
GIRL'S
Book of Prayers

John Lewis Sandlin

FLEMING H. REVELL COMPANY
WESTWOOD • NEW JERSEY

COPYRIGHT © 1966 BY FLEMING H. REVELL COMPANY • ALL RIGHTS
RESERVED • WESTWOOD, NEW JERSEY • LIBRARY OF CONGRESS
CATALOG CARD NUMBER: 66-28004 • PRINTED IN THE UNITED STATES
OF AMERICA • 1.1

To
Sarah Rice Sandlin

PREFACE

We pray because we know God cares and loves and watches over us. In the dawning and at noontide, in the midst of school or work or in recreation, God cares.

Because we know God cares, we, too, can care and know that he loves us as persons. He is with us in the living of the life He gives.

This little book is a guide to our thoughts as we commune with God. Its purpose is the strengthening of relationships between persons and persons and between persons and God.

These prayers are those which relate to the experiences of girls.

J. L. S.

Nashville, Tennessee

A GIRL'S BOOK OF PRAYERS

• PRAISE AND GRATITUDE ✓

Heavenly Father, I praise Thee for all Thy benefits. My gratitude wells up, reminding me to be thankful for Thy love. Thou hast blessed me with health and strengthened my body. Thou hast given me food and clothed me. With understanding, I worship Thee. In Jesus' name. *Amen.*

? COMPASSION ✓

I thank Thee, Lord, for the compassion of Jesus. For the widening fellowship of His love, I am grateful. I would respond to His kindness with thanksgiving for friends and loved ones. Enable me to be truly sympathetic and kind at all times. For Jesus' sake. *Amen.*

• ✓ FOR STRENGTH

O Lord, I seek to be more concerned with expressing thanks for all Thy blessings. Give strength to my faith; help me to look up in praise to Thee for all those unseen benefits. May I be guided by Thy Spirit. Through Christ my Lord. *Amen.*

FOR LIFE'S CHALLENGES

O God, in whom I find resources for living joyously, I thank Thee for the blessing of life. Let me find in this day the challenges that make life meaningful. Show me how to do Thy will. In the Master's name. *Amen.*

FOR UNDERSTANDING

Heavenly Father, help me to keep always a desire to understand. Where I am unable to see through the meaning of things, give me patience, that I may be willing to wait for answers to many questions I cannot answer. In Jesus' name. *Amen.*

FOR THE QUIET PLACE

Dear Lord, I seek the quiet place where hearts are close to one another and to Thee. I seek within the place of rest; I would be still for this moment. Help me to recognize my needs and the needs of others. Renew my thoughts and purify my life. *Amen.*

FOR HOPE

For hope, dear Lord, I pray.
Let me look up today.
Give me new words to say
As now I seek Thy way. *Amen.*

AT BEDTIME

My Father, I believe in Thee;
I trust Thee;
I worship Thee;
I love Thee.
For my wrongdoing I am sorry.
Thou hast been patient and kind to me;
Show me how to love my fellow beings.
Pardon my sins;
Give me grace to follow in Thy way;
Through Jesus Christ my Saviour. *Amen.*

FOR FORGIVENESS

Dear Lord,
   For failure to be kind,
   For lack of regard for others,
   For inability to understand persons,
   For my impatience,
   For my blindness to human need,
Forgive me. *Amen.*

FOR FAITHFULNESS

Lord, let me be aware of my obligation to serve my fellow beings. Let me be faithful to the trust Thou hast placed in me. I dedicate my life to Thee. In the Master's name. *Amen.*

THANKS FOR TIME

O God, in whose sight a thousand years are like an hour passing in the night, I thank You for this day. Help me to use my time as You want it to be employed. Let me be ever watchful of the value of moments as they come. You have blessed me with leisure. Teach me how to use it better for myself and for others. *Amen.*

FOR THIS DAY

For this new day, Dear Lord, I pray;
I seek Thy guidance for the way.
Let me be useful, brave, and kind;
May I be pure in heart and mind. *Amen.*

RENEW MY THOUGHTS

Renew my thoughts, O Lord, I pray;
Lend me a thoughtful mind.
Let me in fellowship obey
In thought and word, in being kind. *Amen.*

FOR KINDNESS

Lord of my life, I would be kind and true to all persons I meet today. Let me be joyful and friendly. Cause me to understand others. Bless all persons everywhere. In Jesus' name. *Amen.*

FOR GRACIOUS WORDS

For gracious words, O Lord, I pray.
Let me speak kindly of each one.
Help me to see the best and speak
The words that are kind.
Make glad every person. *Amen.*

FOR UNDERSTANDING

Gracious Father, who hast given life to be shared, make me affable and kind. Let me live with the assurance of Thy love. May this hour be meaningful. Let me discover ways to worship. May the hours of this day encourage those who need Thy help. In Jesus' name. *Amen.*

FOR TRUST

Help me, O Lord, to leave the anxious moments. Direct me as I try to trust myself. Let me be diligent in studying the lessons I must learn. Fit me for duties and teach me how to trust others. Help me to see Thy plan in all my work. With a glad heart and free from suspicion, I pray. *Amen.*

IN CONFIDENCE AND TRUST

O God, in confidence and trust I come to this time of worship. In Thee alone is my strength. May the unfailing love of Jesus be mine. May I share it. With friendliness and love, in quietness and confidence, I would be true to Thee. In Jesus' name. *Amen.*

FOR PARDON

Dear Lord, I have made mistakes. I have not always followed the best way of doing Thy will. I would obey what I believe is best in Thy sight. Thou hast called me to be diligent in understanding. Help me to meet the challenge of this day. I thank Thee, Lord. *Amen.*

FOR FORGIVENESS

Lord, help me to recognize what I can do in making right decisions. Forgive my wrong acts. Fit me for this day. May I forgive others as Thou dost forgive me. In all the hours of today, help me to share my best. In the Master's name. *Amen.*

FOR THIS DAY

Heavenly Father, in whom I find courage, let me leave behind those anxious thoughts. Enable me to forsake my foolish worries that keep me from doing my best. May I know that each day has enough of its own troubles. Teach me to look ahead with hope and with good humor. For Jesus' sake. *Amen.*

FOR FAIRNESS

Dear Lord, for fairness I pray. Help me to treat others justly. May I be careful in my work; in my recreation, may I have Thy approval. May I be cheerful and considerate and kind in disposition. Teach me how to live in peace. Make me a promoter of friendship. Let me give my thoughts to sincere planning as Thou dost direct me in all things. In the name of Jesus. *Amen.*

BE WITH ME

Be with me, Lord, and keep me pure. Let me be willing to endure the things I must experience, with gladness and with a proper sense of discipline. For Jesus' sake. *Amen.*

FOR SERVICE

Heavenly Father, I am Thine. Let me be willing to serve. Show me how to work with a willing mind and a glad heart. Let me help others. Where I have failed, forgive me. Give strength, that I may overcome my weakness. By the standard of Jesus I would be measured. In His name I pray. *Amen.*

FOR FREEDOM FROM FEAR

Heavenly Father, free me from the unfounded fears. Teach me how to live above littleness and nagging. Be Thou the strength of my life, the Guide of my thoughts. Let me feel Thy nearness in times of joy and gladness. Make me patient in painful experiences. In the brightness of this day, let me be conscious of my opportunity to serve with gladness and with love. Create in my life the power of healthy companionship. In the Master's name. *Amen.*

• FOR KNOWING MYSELF

Teach me how to know myself. Let me be honest in my regard for others. May I recognize my strength and be able to accept my limitations. Help me to find personal power that helps me worship Thee. Inspire me to know when to bring a compliment to another person, and teach me always to be sincere. In the name of Christ. *Amen.*

• FOR JOY IN SERVING

Dear Lord of Life, give me strength to work with gladness and in the spirit of willing service. Give me the pleasure of helping others. Let me remember those to whom I owe the little kindnesses. As I find needy persons, show me how to help them. Let me be unselfish and cheerful. *Amen.*

• FOR THOSE WHO SERVE

Heavenly Father, bless all who serve in various places of responsibility. Let them know that we who enjoy the fruits of their labors are grateful for them and for their efforts. Bless also those "who only stand and wait." In Jesus' name. *Amen.*

FOR DOING RIGHT

Lord of Life, when I have given up a pleasure for conscience' or character's sake, may I be conscious of the greater gain. Let me have Your approval. In power that conquers evil and injustice, may I find the right spirit. I thank You for the joy of knowing Your will in many things. Lead me to the right attitude in all things. In Jesus' name. *Amen.*

PRAYER AT TWILIGHT

Dear Lord, I pause at the close of day to worship Thee. With thanksgiving, I dedicate myself to Thee. Purify my thoughts, that in my meditation I may receive Thy blessing and share it. I am grateful for this time apart from the busy world. For work and play, I thank Thee, Lord. In Jesus' name. *Amen.*

I LIFT MY THOUGHTS

I lift my thoughts to Thee, O Lord. In the coming hours, help me to see my duty and enable me to do it in the best way I can. For Jesus' sake. *Amen.*

• FOR RADIANCE

For a cheerful spirit and for gladness I pray, O Lord. Let me not depend on circumstances for happiness. Help me to remember the words of Jesus, when he said, "My joy I give unto you." And from the words, let me be reassured. I see the meaning of His wonderful spirit in the story of His life. For this I am thankful. Bless all persons who seek to be inspired by His love. In His name. *Amen.*

• FOR GENEROSITY

Teach me, Father, to be generous. Show me how to be kind and charitable, even to those who are unkind. May I be helpful and not difficult. Teach me the art of being kind always. May I compliment the success of others with sincerity. I pray for a right spirit of understanding. Let me share it and receive Thy blessing for having given it freely. In the Master's name. *Amen.*

FOR FREEDOM FROM GRUDGES

Dear Lord, forgive my blunders and mistakes. Forgive my littleness and failure to recognize my own limitations. Let me be free to think clearly. Deliver me from grudges and misunderstandings. Help me to be a friend. Teach me how to recognize the needs of my own life. Give to me the sense of Thy presence. Through Jesus Christ our Lord. *Amen.*

• FOR FAITH

Grant me a steady faith, O Lord;
Let me be guided by Thy word.
Help me to give my heart to Thee
And serve Thee with a mind that's free.
Let me believe in all mankind
And seek Thy love until I find
The meaning of a deeper faith
In living daily as Thou saith. *Amen.*

FOR GOD'S PRESENCE

Let me be conscious of Thy presence, Lord. In the silence of this hour, let me thank Thee for Thy watchful care. I would attend to things that make for friendliness. Let me be gracious to those I meet today. May we abide in Thy presence always. *Amen.*

IN DISAPPOINTMENT

Heavenly Father, I am disappointed. My dream has been shattered. Yet, I know Thou art able to comfort me and inspire me to try again. Help me to reach the goal I've missed. Let me approach the ideal that is set always before me. Let each new experience of disappointment give me courage to begin again. Teach me to be always loyal to Thee. Through Jesus Christ our Lord. *Amen.*

THANKS FOR FORGIVENESS

Heavenly Father, in whom I find forgiveness and in whom my faith is: I thank Thee for the patience and forgiveness of my parents. I am grateful for their forgiveness. I am dependent on Thy love and guidance. Let me see the ways of making others happy in the spirit of the Christian ideal and by the peaceful means. Help me to forgive as Thou hast forgiven me. In the name of Jesus I pray. *Amen.*

AGAINST BITTERNESS

Dear Lord, let no bitterness interrupt my fellowship with Thee. Let no illwill or unkind feeling separate me from any one. Where I am at fault, help me to recognize my shortcomings and make me strong enough to express my regrets.

I ask for forgiveness. Let me not hold grudges toward any person for any reason. Help me to share kindness with all persons I meet. For Jesus' sake. *Amen.*

FOR GUIDANCE

Eternal Father, make me strong enough to bear injuries without thought of "getting even." Let me return good for evil, the smile for the frown, the encouraging words for those who have almost given up the joy of living. May I promote kindness; teach me

how to do Thy will as I am able to find it. In the
Master's name. *Amen.*

LET ME BE KIND

Let me be kind, Dear Lord;
Let me be faithful to your will
In all things, always. *Amen.*

• FOR UNSELFISHNESS

Dear Lord, give me a generous spirit; inspire me to
sacrifice some time for a better tomorrow. Let me not
be selfish. Free me from touchiness. Let me be steady,
devoted to Thy purpose. Help me never to carry a
chip on my shoulder. When life seems difficult, teach
me patience. And let me see the importance of waiting
for a better understanding of others. In Jesus' name.
Amen.

• FOR GOOD WILL

Help me, Dear Lord, always to be friendly with
others. Teach me how to enlarge the circle of friendly
guidance and concern, so that it will be large enough
to include the feeling of good will toward others.
Show me how to be a friend to the unfriendly. Let me
not seek to have my own way. Show me how to listen
to the opinions of others. In the name of Jesus. *Amen.*

AT YEAR'S END

Dear Father, I thank You for the blessings of life, health and strength. I praise You for the things that make life beautiful, my home and friends and playmates. Lead me into the happy places today and use me to share cheerful thoughts. In the Master's name. *Amen.*

HAPPINESS AT YEAR'S END

The year is ended, Lord. I am so happy to be a person among others. You have given so many privileges to me during the last year. Let me share my opportunities with others. Bless all who call on You and help each one to be thoughtful of others. *Amen.*

NEW YEAR'S

Heavenly Father, for another year I thank you. For another dawn of day, I am glad. For another look at the beautiful world Thou hast made, I am grateful. I want to be useful in all ways today. Let me find the friends I need and the strength to do Thy will as I am able to discover it. In Jesus' name. *Amen.*

FOR EPIPHANY

Heavenly Father, You guided the Wise Men by the Star of Bethlehem. Guide me. Let me share Your love.

Let me think of the baby Jesus as the central person in a home. Bless my home and show me how to bring happy experiences to those who live here. Let me give myself in earnest effort to find the way to goals of service. In Jesus' name. *Amen.*

• FOR DOING MY BEST

O Lord, the call of Jesus comes clearly to my heart. I would follow Him as He shows the way to obeying Thy will. May I become better than I am. Create in me a clean heart and renew my understanding of the way that is in the spirit of compassionate resourcefulness. This I ask in the name of Jesus. *Amen.*

FOR THE GIFT OF TIME

Dear Lord, I thank You for time. It is life to me, the power of love. You have given me thoughts and enabled me to see the way to serve. Make me useful in this wonderful day You have given. In the name of Jesus. *Amen.*

FOR CALMNESS

For calmness and serenity, Dear Lord, I pray. Let me find here the strength I need for life. In mind and heart I would seek to be quiet. May I do the best I can with a willing mind and a pure heart. Abide in my heart and give strength to my desire for fellowship. I thank You for this quiet time. Let me be quiet. I thank You for the serenity of His life. In His name I pray. *Amen.*

FOR FORGIVENESS

Heavenly Father, forgive my failure to be diligent; help me to recognize my opportunities for making life meaningful to others. In the name of Christ. *Amen.*

FOR PLEASING MANNERS

Dear Lord, may I meet the day with an open smile and a strong faith. Let me be cheerful. Make me able to receive the training in improvment that I need. Teach me how to regard the rights of others as I think about my own; give right direction to the thoughts I have of my growing concern for doing what You would have me do. In the name of Jesus. *Amen.*

FOR PURE AIMS

Lord, let me think and plan and serve in the right way. I do not always know the direction, but you can teach me. I am willing to learn and ready to listen to those who give instruction. Let me feel the nearness of Thy Holy Spirit. Forgive my wandering attitude.

Let me give attention to improving the way I do things. Help me to plan beyond my knowledge and strive to reach new goals. For Christ's sake. *Amen.*

TEACH ME, LORD

Teach me, Lord, that I may serve with improving skills. Let me dedicate all I am and all I have to Thy service. *Amen.*

FOR TRUSTWORTHINESS

Lord, help me to prove the trust I have in Thee. Let me be trustworthy. Show me how to do my work with the sincere effort that is important and my privilege to do. In all the day's activities, I would share the meaning of each moment as it brings out the best in my life. In the Master's name. *Amen.*

FOR PERSEVERANCE

Heavenly Father, sometimes I am discouraged. I do not know where to turn for help. Let me put my trust in Thee. May I keep watch over the spiritual meaning of this day. Help me to serve with a glad heart. Continue to bless all who hold on to duties you have given. Let me serve, even under handicap, in the spirit of understanding and with love. For Jesus' sake. *Amen.*

• LET ME LOVE

Lord, let me love the dawning of this day; let me give myself to the things that cause others to love Thee and those whom Thou hast made. For Jesus' sake. *Amen.*

FOR FAITH ✓

Lord, I believe in Thee. I seek to be strong in faith. Let me be faithful to the trust Thou hast given me. Help me to understand my work and responsibility. In confidence and with a pure heart, I would be peaceful in association with others. Let me think noble thoughts and plan deeds of goodness. In Jesus' name. *Amen.*

FOR GUIDANCE ✓

Dear Lord, guide me through this day and help me to find the way to right decisions. Show me how to decide what is right. Help me to seek right ways. For Thy guidance I am grateful. Make me strong. Bless my plans. In the name of Christ. *Amen.*

LET ME DO RIGHT ✓

Help me, Dear Lord, to do the right;
Let me be faithful now.
Grant me the proper word to say
When in Thy presence now I bow. *Amen.*

MORNING PRAYER

This is the day Thou hast made, O Lord. Let me rejoice and be glad in it. This is the time for making a beginning. Let me find strength in Thee. O Lord, give me a new view of the meaning of time and help me to use it as I feel be pleasing to Thee. May I give thought to things that are important. In the Master's name. *Amen.*

BEGINNING THE DAY

Dear Lord, for this day I am thankful. It is new and unspoiled; show me how to keep it that way. In the morning light, may I see that you care for us. In school, at work, or in leisure hours, keep me close to Thee. For Jesus' sake. *Amen.*

FOR THIS DAY

For this new day, I thank Thee. For light and sunny hours and time for play, I thank Thee. For friends and loved ones, for those who care, I am grateful. Let me so live that my life will please Thee. For the Master's sake. *Amen.*

MORNING PRAYERS

Be with me now, Dear Lord,
  At dawn and through the day;
Teach me to say each word
  That helps me now to pray. *Amen.*

I seek Thee, Lord, today,
  While dew is on the grass;
I find Thee in the dawn
  Of day as shadows pass. *Amen.*

I look again to Thee:
  With pure delight, I see
Thy beauty all around;
  It is a lovely sight. *Amen.*

So fill my heart with love
  For persons everywhere,
That I may look above
  And share Thy tender care. *Amen.*

Let me be kind and true;
  Forgive my every fault.
Let me my hope renew
  As Thy name I exalt. *Amen.*

IN ANXIOUS MOMENTS

Heavenly Father, in my anxious moments, help me
to see the way through. Let me be patient with myself
and with others, believing where I am unable to see.
Help me to think in sincerity. Give me confidence in
the outcome of this and other experiences that hold
me back from doing my best. In Thee I put my trust.
In Jesus' name. *Amen.*

FREEDOM FROM GOSSIP

Lord, help me to be free from the sin of gossip. Let me keep silent when I should and speak up when it would be possible to rescue another from the destruction of slander.

Free me from all idle talk and besmirching language. Let me be pure in attitude and in word, as well as in deed. Forgive those times when I have neglected to keep silent. Where I can be helpful, help me to be kind and prompt in making the best effort. For Jesus' sake. *Amen.*

FOR ORDERLINESS

Thine, O Lord, is this day. Thou hast given daylight. Thou hast commanded light to come out of darkness. Everything Thou hast made points to order and design. I would seek to be orderly and careful in my plans. Let me be aware of arranging my life as Thou wouldst have it. Forgive my slow ways. Make me strong to obey what I know is right. In Jesus' name. *Amen.*

GOD IS MY STRENGTH

Bless me with health and strength, O Lord. Grant that I may find ways to serve. Show me how to live. Let me be true to the best and highest way of doing all that I find to do. Help me to make right choices.

May I try to learn what is right. And when the day is done, make me able to rest. Let me overcome my difficult problems. Give me courage to face my studies with determination and hope. In the name of Jesus I pray. *Amen.*

• FOR HONESTY

I would be honest, Lord: honest with myself and honest with others. But most of all, let me be honest with Thee. For Jesus' sake. *Amen.*

• FOR TRUST AND CONFIDENCE

Almighty God, who hast given me life, may I be faithful in daily living. Teach me to trust others. Let me believe in others and give them confidence and encouragement. In noble thinking I would be diligently engaged. In Thee I trust. For Jesus' sake. *Amen.*

SO MUCH IS GIVEN

O God, You have given me so much more than I deserve! You have blessed me with so many of life's extras! I am grateful for them all. You have made a home for my family and made love the center. As I come to thank You for all these blessings, I rejoice. Let me follow the teachings of the Master. In His name I pray. *Amen.*

FOR PROPER USE OF MONEY

Dear Lord, I do not have much money to share. But I want to use it as You want me to use it. Let me know how to be generous without being careless. Let me be thrifty without being stingy. Let me be faithful in all the spending I do. For Jesus' sake. *Amen.*

FOR CLEANSING

O Lord, cleanse me from selfishness. Let me be kind and gracious to those I meet. Free me from being cross or unpleasant. Enable me to be sincere and pure. Give to me a concern for others, that I may help in making life happy for them. Let me face life with purity and grace. In the Master's name. *Amen.*

WHEN TRAVELING

O Lord, I desire to be renewed by the experiences I have on this trip. There are so many beautiful sites. Let me share the wonder of the road, the beauty of the trees and flowers. Give me safe journey and help me to discern the meaning of Thy creation as it appears in the places I visit. Bless those with whom I travel. Keep them safe and sound in all the journey. And when we are ready to return home, let us find rest. For Jesus' sake. *Amen.*

FOR TRUSTFULNESS

Heavenly Father, I do love Thee. I would try to recognize Thee in this time of worship. May I explore every dark nook of my life with Thy love as the torch to light the way. Help me to trust in Thee through all difficulties. When the road of life seems to be blocked or jammed with obstacles, make me strong in courage and steadfast in hope. I would believe beyond the place of sight; I would discover beyond the possible; I would be loving where it would seem that love is impossible. Let me possess the reassurance of the trustful outlook in life. Through Jesus Christ my Lord. *Amen.*

FOR REASSURANCE

O Lord, reach into my life with Thy cleansing power. By Thy consolation and blessing, I am made whole. Thy tenderness has taught me to be sympathetic. Thy fatherly goodness lifts me closer to others. I am grateful for this relationship.

May I have the reassuring love that guides and directs all who follow Thee. And as the day wears on, may I not wear thin in patience. May I maintain an attitude of longsuffering and kindness. This I ask in the name of Him who came to bring abundant life. *Amen.*

✦ THOU MASTER OF LIFE

Thou Master of the trails of life,
　　In whom I find my best,
Show me the way beyond all strife,
　　And grant me quiet rest.

Support me now and every day,
　　And help me to be kind;
Make glad my heart as now I say
　　A prayer for all I find.

Thou Master of the trails of life,
　　Make me a child of Thine;
Remove my attitudes of strife,
　　And all my life refine. *Amen.*

✦ FOR EXCELLENCE

Lord, show me the duties that are mine. Help me to know how to improve the work I am doing. Give me strength to think amidst the new duties. Let me work for excellence. Bring forth the power I need for laying new plans to fill the hours with gladness. May I have grace to carry out the plans I have made. Remove my complacency, and help me to improve my work. In the name of Jesus. *Amen.*

FOR FELLOWSHIP

Dear Lord, I long for fellowship with those who in this quiet nook have lingered silently and sought ways in which to serve their fellow beings. I wait with gladness and with love for the assurance of Thy peace. Help me to wait with patience and understanding. In the spirit of the Master. *Amen.*

GOD'S PRESENCE

Dear Heavenly Father, I wait here and know Thou art present. I am a needy child of Thine. I am ready to do whatever Thou wilt show me how to do. Bless others and use me to bless them, too. *Amen.*

THANKS FOR TODAY

Dear Lord, I thank You for today. I am glad to be alive and well. Let me give my thoughts to the best You would lead me toward. Grant that I may serve in ways that are meaningful to others. For Christ's sake. *Amen.*

LET ME BE KIND

Let me be kind, O Lord. Give me the attitude of love toward all persons. Fill my heart with loving-kindness and compassion. *Amen.*

SEEKING GOD

I seek Thee, Lord, today,
    While the dew is on the grass;
And I find Thee in the dawning
    As the fading shadows pass. *Amen.*

FOR PURITY

Heavenly Father, in whom I find strength, help me
to be always pure in heart and self-respecting. May I
hold high the thoughts and dreams of each new experience. Thou hast created me in Thy image. Teach me
to be always loyal to Thee. In Jesus' name. *Amen.*

FOR DEDICATION

O Lord, to Thee my life I dedicate. To Thee I
would be true. Help me to give my best effort to doing
the things I believe you would have me do. May my
thoughts and dreams be acceptable in Thy sight. For
Thy dear sake. *Amen.*

AN EVENING PRAYER

The evening comes again, Dear Lord;
    The day has long since passed.
I look to Thee for each new word
    Of reassurance that will last. *Amen.*

FOR CHEERFULNESS

Help me, dear Lord, to be cheerful and sincere and loyal to the ideal and the beautiful. May the reflection of good humor be my possession. Through this new day, help me to express the pleasing attitude that will draw persons closer to one another and closer to Thee. *Amen.*

FOR SYMPATHY

Heavenly Father, grant me a sympathetic attitude. Teach me how to share the spirit of understanding, the fellowship of love. May I be always willing to give with no thought of receiving in return. Inspire me to be alert to the needs of others, that I may bring a message of comfort, a word of encouragement. In Jesus' name. *Amen.*

FOR FAITHFULNESS

Let me be faithful, Lord. Let me be ever true to the best I know. I need the steadiness of Thy love to inspire, the constancy of Thy Spirit to give hope, the loveliness of good fellowship to make life worthwhile. May I remain true to the ideal to which Thou hast called me. In the name of Jesus. *Amen.*

FOR LOVE

Heavenly Father,
    So fill my heart with love
      For persons everywhere,
That I may look above
      And share Thy tender care. *Amen.*

FOR KINDNESS

Heavenly Father, help me to be considerate of others. May I so regard and respect their feelings that they may never suffer because of any careless word of mine. May I hold in high regard my fellow beings. Guide me by the attitude of Jesus, in whose name I pray. *Amen.*

GIVING THANKS

For the consciousness of Thy nearness,
For the blessing of life and its benefits,
For the love of friends who say a cheerful word,
For so many evidences of Thy love and care,
    I give Thee thanks, O Lord. *Amen.*

FOR FAITHFULNESS

O Lord, help me to encourage those I meet. Show me how to be faithful to the trust that is mine through increasing responsibility. Increase my insight and let

me find the place of service in obedience to Thy call.
In Jesus' name. *Amen.*

✓ FOR A KIND DISPOSITION

Heavenly Father, whose love abides with all who
seek Thy guidance: bless me with a kind disposition.
Enable me to be steady in mind, cheerful and thoughtful. Strengthen my faith that I may share courage with
others. In Thy name. *Amen.*

✓ FOR A FORWARD LOOK

Lord, let me live this day with a forward look and
a consciousness of Thy presence. So fill my thoughts
with gratitude for all Thy goodness that in the coming
day my attitude will be acceptable in Thy sight. Teach
me how to bring my best thinking to the living of this
day. In the Master's name. *Amen.*

✓ FOR COURAGE

Help me to see beyond the clouds of disappointment.
Although the way seems dark, help me to learn to wait
with patience for the dawning of the light of reinforc-
ing hope. Let me find courage to keep alive the embers
of the forward look. Bring me to the living fellowship
of growing understanding and good will. May the

constancy of Thy Spirit guide me to the goal of brotherhood. In Jesus' name I pray. *Amen.*

✓ FOR TOMORROW

Lord, let me see beyond today
The beauty of tomorrow;
Let me to others bring, I pray,
A word of gladness for their sorrow. *Amen.*

✓ FOR FORGIVENESS

Dear Father, in love and trust I lift my thoughts to Thee. I ask forgiveness for my own indifference to Thy will. Make real to me the meaning of Thy sacrificial love. May I share the compassion of our blessed Lord. In His name I pray. *Amen.*

✓ FOR RESOURCEFULNESS

O Lord, renew my thoughts, that I may be creative and resourceful. Help me to bring hope to the lonely. Show me the way to inspire joy and steadfastness in the lives of others. May the cheerfulness of a smile become my possession; make glad my heart, that I may share the meaning of the cheerfulness of Christ who went about doing good. In His name I pray. *Amen.*

FOR HIGH STANDARDS

Gracious Father, as I approach this hour of worship, help me to hold my standards high. Let me not compromise with selfishness and prejudice. Let me follow in the way Thou dost direct me. In all I try to do, help me to be renewed in spirit and in faith. In the name of Jesus. *Amen.*

FOR SHARING LOVE

Gracious Father, whose love is my assurance and whose truth is my salvation: help me humbly to understand Thy matchless love. Show me how to share it with neighbors and friends and all others I may meet today. Create within my heart a continual attitude of cooperation with all who seek Thy purpose. *Amen.*

FOR A RIGHT SPIRIT

O God, on this day I come seeking a knowledge of Thy will and purpose for my life. Teach me so to cherish the love which Thou hast given, that I may exalt Thy goodness in all I think and say and do. In Jesus' name. *Amen.*

A BENEDICTION

Dear Lord, let me find rest in the assurance of Thy presence here and now and always. In the name of Jesus. *Amen.*

DAY AND NIGHT: A MEDITATION

A day of wonder, yet serene,
With azure clouds and light between,
A sight of beauty to behold
Reminds me of Thy love untold.
The lingering light of setting sun
Delays the shadows just begun;
Still, I can see a winding rill
Beyond the shadow of the hill;
And now I know, above the night,
Thy light is shining pure and bright.

FOR A NEW LIFE

Dear Lord, I now accept Jesus Christ as my Saviour and Lord. Help me to lead a new life, following Thy commandments and walking from henceforth in Thy holy way. With love and charity for my neighbors, may I determine to be what Thou wouldst have me be. In Jesus' name. *Amen.*

FOR LOVE

Let love abide with us today
And bind us close to Thee;
Let all who worship find the way
To Him who sets us free. *Amen.*

FOR FORGIVENESS

Dear Lord of life, who art the source of love, come into my life that I may share the glad tidings of great joy. In Christ we seek to be renewed. By Him we come to share the meaning of Thy steadfast love. Forgive my misdeeds and strengthen me in the attitude of forgiveness. In Jesus' name. *Amen.*

FOR CONSTANCY

Lord, help me to live with constancy. Let me be diligent and kind in all relationships. In moments yet to come, invest my thoughts with the spirit of Jesus, in whose name I pray. *Amen.*

● FOR ENDURANCE

Dear Father, help me to endure the situations I can not change. With calmness and patience I would follow Thee. If I must suffer, let me be calm and hopeful and quiet. Let me be faithful to Thy trust and loyal to the promises I make. Forgive my slowness in recognizing the value in the things I must accept. In Jesus' name. *Amen.*

GRATITUDE

Heavenly Father, I am grateful for the blessing of life, the privilege of work, and the steadiness of Thy love. May I be willing to obey Thy purpose as I am able to understand and discover it. In the Master's name. *Amen.*

FOR A LOVELY DAY

For another day, I thank Thee, Lord. For flowers and sunshine and the song of birds, I am thankful. May the glory of this place remind me to be gracious. Help me to bring unity of spirit into this time of living. Thou art the Source of all that is alive and vibrant with eternal goodness. Help me to recognize Thy presence here and now and always. *Amen.*

GOD'S PRESENCE

In blooming flowers and singing birds,
　　In pleasant memories dear,
In lovely dreams and kindly words,
　　I find Thy presence here. *Amen.*

GOD'S PRESENCE AT EVENTIDE

Dear Lord,
　　Be with me—linger and abide!
　　Lift up my thoughts at eventide!
　　I would be listening now to Thee,
　　The One whose love surroundeth me. *Amen.*

● AT CLOSE OF DAY

Heavenly Father, darkness reminds me now of quiet rest. The stillness of the twilight hour has blessed me with Thy presence. I thank Thee for the softness of the shadows, the silent watches of the night, and the thoughts of plans for tomorrow. I pray that Thy will be done in my life. In Jesus' name. *Amen.*

● THANKS FOR REST

I thank you, Lord, for rest. I am tired now, but I know that You will give rest for another day's activities. When morning breaks and the sun appears, I will give thanks for every blessing. In the name of Christ. *Amen.*

✕ FOR LOYALTY

Lord, for the blessing of this day,
  I thank Thee now;
Help me, dear Lord, to laugh and grow
  And humbly bow.

Lord, let me give myself
  In loyalty;
Teach me the way of love
  As now I bow.

Grant that I now may serve
    Unselfishly;
Lord, lift my sights above the din
    Of all strife today. *Amen.*

● FOR WISDOM

Dear Lord of life and truth and hope,
Thou Guardian of the trackless way,
Teach me new wisdom as I cope
With difficulties through this day.
Help me to share the light of love
And ever in good humor move. *Amen.*

● THANKS FOR FRIENDS

Lord, let me remember to be thankful for friends who have made life meaningful. Let me see in the helpfulness of others an expression of Thy goodness, a living witness of Thy fellowship. *Amen.*

● FOR PROPER WORTH

Heavenly Father, who art the One in whom I find the best, help me to recognize the best in others. May I be fair in my treatment of others. Let me find in persons the meaning of good living and beautiful acting. I would be true in making life less difficult for those I serve. I look to Thee for guidance. Bless all who follow high ideals. In the Master's name. *Amen.*

● FOR UNSELFISHNESS

Teach me, Dear Lord, how to live above the fog of selfishness. Direct my thinking that I may be considerate of those I live among. Bless us with understanding of one another. In Jesus' name. *Amen.*

● FOR HONESTY

For honesty, Dear Lord, I pray. May I be true to high ideals. In times of difficulty and severe trial, enable me to speak with frankness and to mean it. So may I live that I may be self-respecting and pure. In thought I would be clean; in word I would be accurate; in deed I would be faithful to every trust given to me. *Amen.*

● FOR SPIRITUAL STRENGTH

Teach me, my Father God, to see
The person that I ought to be;
Let me be strengthened as I strive
Thy will to do and keep alive. *Amen.*

● FOR GENEROSITY

All that is mine is Thine, O Lord;
Whatever I have is a gift from Thee.
Help me to share it as I see
It as an offering given to Thee. *Amen.*

⚜ FOR HELPFULNESS

May I be helpful, Lord. Where there is need, use me to help supply it. As I am able to be resourceful, help me so to be. Help me to be more diligent in service. In Jesus' name. *Amen.*

⚜ FOR A CLEAR MIND

Dear Lord, I pray for a clear mind. May I know how to guide my emotions by calmness and reason. Let me be faithful to the work Thou hast given me to do. Guide my steps aright. In temptation, help me to keep faith with Thee in all things, always. For Jesus' sake. *Amen.*

⚜ FOR OVERCOMING TEMPTATION

O God, deliver me from the pitfalls of temptation. Lift my thoughts above the evil that tempts me. Preserve me from dangers that would destroy my ideals. For Jesus' sake. *Amen.*

⚜ FOR SELF-CONTROL

For self-control, Dear Lord, I pray. May I be calm in spirit and clear in mind. Let me be steady, able to experience Thy presence, and ready to possess reassurance. Give me courage to speak at the right time. May

I do right. Show me how to control my emotions. For Thy sake. *Amen.*

AN EVENING PRAYER

Lord, help me to remain serene and sure of Thy protection. The day has been beautiful. May the night be restful and refreshing. Bless me as I go to rest. Forgive my misdeeds. Strengthen my body and grant me kind thoughts. Make me able to serve with gladness in the coming day. *Amen.*

FOR PURITY

Dear Lord, keep me pure and clean,
Let me be thoughtful and serene.
I would be loyal, too, as now
I seek Thy will to do.
In Jesus' name. *Amen.*

FOR CHEERFULNESS

Lord, may the happiness I feel be shared with those I meet today. Let me give a cheerful word. At home, at school, or in time of recreation, teach me to be joyful and helpful and hopeful. May I be kind. Let me pass on to others a smile and a word of cheer. *Amen.*

FOR FAIRNESS

Dear Lord, teach me to be faithful always. Free me from grudges. In my meeting with others, I would be kind. Remove all hatred and littleness. Let me be free from any desire to have what others own. Let me be fair in all associations. *Amen.*

FOR POISE

Dear Lord, I pray for calmness. In disturbing situations, help me to be composed and steady. Remove my sense of insecurity, that I may find in Christ the experience of a growing faith, a steady hope, a purpose for living. I pause for spiritual renewal. For Jesus' sake. *Amen.*

FOR GUIDANCE

I thank Thee, Lord, for guiding me to this place of worship. I am grateful for the fellowship of those who have helped me in forming good habits. Let me be constant in devotion to Thee and to the doing of Thy will. May I find strength for being useful. In the name of Jesus. *Amen.*

FOR STEADINESS

Heavenly Father, may this day be one in which love and devotion shall prevail. Enlighten me with the love of my fellow beings. Help me to remain loyal to the trust you have given me. Let me give my best in all relationships. Through Jesus Christ my Lord. *Amen.*

FOR APPRECIATION

Lord, let me be conscious of the beauty all about the countryside. I thank Thee for eyes to see; help me to appreciate it. Let me be grateful for all you have given me to enjoy. *Amen.*

FOR DEDICATION

Almighty God, unto whom my heart is open, all my dreams known, and from whom nothing can be hid: I dedicate my life to Thee. In Jesus' name. *Amen.*

• DEDICATION

Teach me, O Lord, to be my best:
    To smile and not to frown,
    To be courageous and not cowardly,
    To be diligent and not careless,
    To be kind and never harsh.
Let me dedicate myself to the accomplishment of the goals that are before me. *Amen.*

• FOR COURAGE

O God of love, I turn away from the noise and confusion of the busy world, looking to Thee for strength. I need courage for the tasks of this day. In faith I look forward to my work. May Thy love abide with all who turn to Thee for guidance. In the Master's name. *Amen.*

• FOR PEACE

O God of peace, in whom I trust, help me to be quiet. Let me listen for the still small voice within. Thou art speaking to me through the silence. May I share with others the grace of unselfish commitment to the purposes which promote harmony and peaceful atitudes. May the grace of an unselfish commitment to Christ be the possession of all who look to Thee for guidance. In the name of the Prince of Peace. *Amen.*

• IN TIME OF SORROW

O Lord, my heart is touched by sadness. The loneliness of this hour is great, yet I know that Thou art able to make less the pain of my suffering. I come to Thee remembering the words of Jesus when he said, "Come to me all who labor and are heavy laden and I will give you rest." Help me to bear the strain with patience and courage. Let me be comforted in the assurance of Thy love. In the Saviour's name. *Amen.*

• FOR CONSOLATION

Lord, give consolation to all who suffer. Comfort those who sorrow. May Thy blessing abide with those who are in need of Thy comfort. May the guidance of Thy Spirit live in our hearts. In Jesus' name. *Amen.*

FOR HAPPINESS

Dear Lord, who hast given happiness to light my way, let me make others joyful. Teach me how to bring gladness and joy. Show me how to hold the spirit of optimism and faith. May I ever keep in remembrance the joyful experience of fellowship with friends of yesterday. In Thy dear name. *Amen.*

FOR FORGIVENESS

Dear Father, let love abide in my heart and shed abroad its benefits. Let kindness live among us as we share the loveliness of Thy blessings. Forgive us for any unkind thoughts and pardon our failure to recognize our dependence on each other and on Thee. For Jesus' sake. *Amen.*

FOR HARMONY

Heavenly Father, I pray for harmony in my relationships. Give me courage to face the difficulties of life with steadiness and faith. Let me be calm in spirit as I try to share the kindly attitude of Jesus. In His name I pray. *Amen.*

MY HEART'S DESIRE

My heart's desire and prayer to Thee, O Lord,
Is that today may find me close to Thee.
My dream of goals of service I would share
With those who are reminded of Thy care.

Lift high my thoughts of Thy redeeming love;
Let me be useful and resourceful as I move
Into the closer fellowship of Christ my Friend,
That I may remain faithful to the end. *Amen.*

FOR PATIENCE

Heavenly Father, when I am restless and tired and impatient, I need reassurance. Teach me how to remain calm and faithful. Let the serenity of Thy Spirit guide my thoughts. May the quiet attitude of Jesus remind me to be silent. As I ponder the meaning of Thy love for all persons everywhere, let me be patient. For Jesus' sake. *Amen.*

• FOR LIFE AND WORK

Lord, let me live and work
And serve with willing mind;
Let me discover in this day
The strength for each new step along my way.
Let me be faithful to each task
And give my best and nothing ask. *Amen.*

• FOR TRUST

Dear Lord of life, help me to see that my concern is part of Thy great design. May I be conscious of Thy love for all that is in my life in growth and in purpose. Teach me to trust the future to Thy care. May I live this day with gladness and hope. Forgive my fretfulness, my failure to trust my problems to Thy care. In Thy keeping I place my life. In the name of Jesus. *Amen.*

• FOR HUMILITY

Lord, let me know when to be retiring in attitude and when to speak out. May my manner of conversation never be unfair or domineering. In humble trust, let me be courteous and friendly to all persons. May Thy love abide in the fellowship that unites us. Through Jesus Christ our Lord. *Amen.*

• FOR VISION

Heavenly Father, help me to see beyond the material world. Let me perceive that in thoughts of the future there is power of spirit to be shared. By this unseen, yet real, experience of growing fellowship, help me to reach for higher goals in service to be done. I would be ever watchful for new tasks, new ways of doing things. *Amen.*